D0674004

WITHDRAWN FROM
THE NEELB LIBRARY SERVICE
ON....................
FOR SALE AT

LIBRARIES NI
WITHDRAWN FROM STOCK

STARTING
PAINTING

Susan Mayes

Designed by Lindy Dark

Illustrated by Terry Burton

Photographs by Howard Allman

Art consultant: Gill Figg

Series editor: Cheryl Evans

With thanks to Shelley Gibbins

NORTH EASTERN LIBRARY SERVI
AREA LIBRARY, DEMESNE AVENUE
BALLYMENA, Co. ANTRIM BT43 7BG
NUMBER 7057685
CLASS J751 • 4

Contents

Things you need

This book shows you how to use paint in lots of ways. There are plenty of ideas for things to paint and make using the new skills you learn. On these pages you can see the things you need. You can buy them from an art shop or a good stationer's.

Paints

There are different kinds of paints. The best ones to use for the projects in this book are ready-mixed paint, powder paint or acrylic paint.

Ready-mixed paint

Powder paint

Acrylic paint

Water-colour paints, oil paints and blocks of paint are not good for the projects in this book.

Colours

You need a red, a blue, a yellow, white and black. You may have different reds, blues and yellows to choose from. Pick a red called crimson if you have a choice.

If you like, buy an extra red, blue or yellow.

Thickener

You can make paint thicker by mixing in a thickener called PVA glue. Add a little to powder paints or liquid paints. (See page 12.)

PVA glue looks white until you mix it in.

Don't get any on your clothes as it is difficult to get out.

What to paint on

You may like to buy new paper to use. It comes in different sizes. You need A4 size or A3 size for most of the things in this book.

You could buy bigger pieces and cut them to the size you need.

A3 is 42x29.7cm (16½x11¾in)

A4 is 21x29.7cm (8¼x11¾in)

You can use white or coloured paper.

Sketchbook

A sketchbook has blank pages that you can paint, draw or stick on.
It is useful for testing colours and trying out ideas.

Find out how to make your own sketchbook on pages 24 and 25.

Brushes

Brushes come in different sizes. Some have soft bristles and some have stiff bristles. It is best to have three soft brushes, for different kinds of painting.

Medium-thickness

Thin, for delicate work

Thick, for painting big areas

A medium-thickness stiff brush is useful, too.

Extra things

You need these extra things every time you paint.

Short plastic pots or a plastic palette, to put paint in

A short jar and a flat plate

Newspaper

Paper kitchen towel or a rag

An old shirt or an apron

Before you start

Clear a big space and spread out lots of newspaper.

Collect the things in the list at the beginning of the project and the things shown above.

Put your painting shirt on and fill the jar with clean water.

Make a folder

You could make a folder to put your paintings in. Stick two big sheets of cardboard together with sticky tape. Use sheets that are bigger than A3 size.

You could decorate the folder.

3

Experimenting

You can paint with brushes, but you can use other things too. Collect at least ten different tools that you could paint marks with. Here are some ideas.

Preparing paint

Different sorts of paint need preparing in different ways to make them a good thickness for painting with.

Ready-mixed paint comes ready to use. So does acrylic paint in tubs or bottles.

Acrylic paint in tubes is quite thick.

Powder paint is dry until you add water to it.

Don't fill the pot.

To use ready-mixed paint or acrylic paint in tubs or bottles, just put the colour you need in its own pot.

Always put the paint in before the water.

Use a dry spoon

To use powder paint, spoon some into a pot. Drip a few drops of clean water on from a brush. Mix it all in.

Always use clean water for mixing.

To use acrylic paint in tubes, squeeze some into a pot. Mix in drops of water to make the paint creamy.

A lid stops the paint from drying out quickly.

If you have some paint left over when you finish painting, put the pots in a plastic tub with a lid on.

Making marks

Things you need:
Three colours of paint
A big sheet of paper
A collection of tools
for making marks
A plate

Use different
parts of
each tool.

Prepare a colour. Put some
on the plate with a brush,
then dip a tool in.

You could
write the
name of the
thing you used
beside each mark.

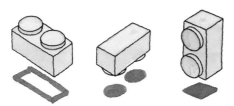

See how many ways you
can use the tool to paint
marks on the paper.

Which tools
makes the biggest
number of
different marks?

**Brush paint
onto big tools.**

Change the colour you use
each time you choose a
new tool.

Cleaning tips

Always change the water
in the jar if it gets dirty
while you are painting.

Clean each tool when
you have finished
making marks with it.

Wash everything up at the
end, to get the paint off.

5

Making new colours

Red, yellow and blue are called primary colours. You can mix them in different ways to make new colours.

Things you need:
White paper
A pencil and a ruler
Thin wax crayons
(not chunky ones)
Paints
A thin brush
Scissors

1

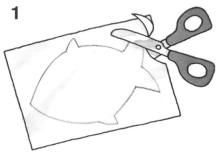

Draw a fat fish shape on the paper and cut it out. Make the fish about 20cm (8in) long.

2

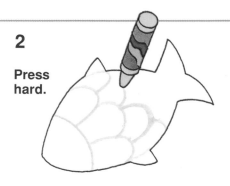

Press hard.

Draw a pattern on the fish with a yellow wax crayon. The pattern needs about 14 shapes in it.

3

Always wash out the brush and dry it on a rag.

Prepare red and yellow paint in pots. Use a brush to put some yellow on a plate. Paint one shape on the fish.

4

Paint a shape next to the first one.

Add a spot of red to the yellow on the plate. Mix the colours together. Paint a shape with the new colour.

5

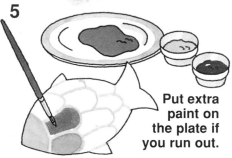

Put extra paint on the plate if you run out.

Add a little more red to the colour you mixed to change it again. Paint a new shape. Keep making new colours.

Powder paint

If the powder won't disappear, add a tiny drop of water.

Dry powder paint in pots

Dip a damp brush in the yellow powder. Mix it around on the plate. Wash and dry the brush. Then mix in some red.

If you can't make any more colours and your fish has empty spaces, try mixing colours to match ones you have made already.

Can you make a different colour for each shape?

A colour made by mixing two primary colours is called a secondary colour.

6

More colours

Use a blue crayon to draw a pattern on another fish. Mix yellow and blue to make lots of new colours.

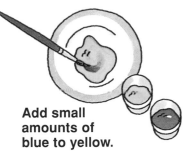

Add small amounts of blue to yellow.

Cut out a new fish. Draw a pattern with a blue crayon. Mix red and blue to make as many colours as you can.

Start with red, then add blue to it.

Make about 14 spaces on each fish.

Use a black crayon to draw a pattern on another fish. Add tiny amounts of black to white and paint the shapes.

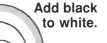

Add black to white.

Three-colour mix

You can mix yellow, blue and red to make brown. Start with yellow and add small amounts of red and blue. What happens if you add more of one colour than another?

This brown has more blue in it.

This brown has more red in it.

This brown has more yellow in it.

Colour blends

Painting colours so they mix into each other is called blending. The picture below has a blended background.

On these pages you need:
A4 size white paper
Paints
Thick and thin soft brushes
A big potato
A scrap of cardboard
Scissors
A rag or paper towel

Dark to light

Thick brush

Paint all the way across.

Prepare blue and white in pots. If you use powder paint, add water to it. Put some of the blue on a plate.

Lay the paper with its short edges at the sides. Paint a blue band across the top. Clean the brush in water.

Work quickly before the paint dries.

Brush the join to make it disappear.

The lightness or darkness of a colour is called its tone.

Primary blends

Yellow and red blend

Red and blue blend

Yellow and blue blend

Blend primary colours by following the steps on the left. Use two colours instead of blue and white.

Mix some white into the blue on the plate, to make it lighter. Paint a band slightly overlapping the first one.

Mix more white into the blue and paint another band. Make each band lighter than the last one, until you finish.

Sailing boats

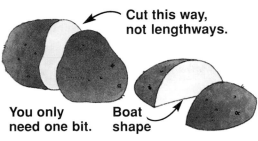

Cut this way, not lengthways.

You only need one bit.

Boat shape

Sail shape underneath

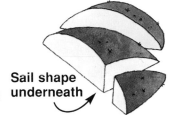

Cut a potato in half. Put one half with its cut side facing down. Cut it in half again. Ask an adult to help.

Take the bit left over from the boat shape. Cut a bit off the bottom. Cut off the curved side.

Paint a blue blend with a thick brush. Then turn the paper the other way around and leave it to dry.

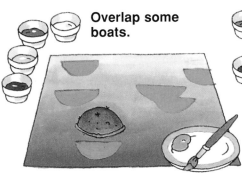

Overlap some boats.

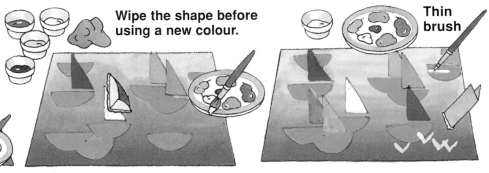

Wipe the shape before using a new colour.

Thin brush

Mix a colour for the boats. Paint the boat shape and press it onto the paper. Do lots of boats like this.

Print a coloured sail on each boat. Start on the boats at the top, then work your way down the paper.

Fold a strip of cardboard lengthways. Dip the end in white paint and print waves. Paint lines on the boats.

Colour-blend painting

You can do lots of different colour blends in a painting. Blend pairs of colours, or blend a colour and white.

On these pages you need:

A3 white paper
Paint
Medium-thickness soft brush
Things to draw around
Pencil and ruler
Scissors and glue stick
Self-adhesive plastic
A3 cardboard

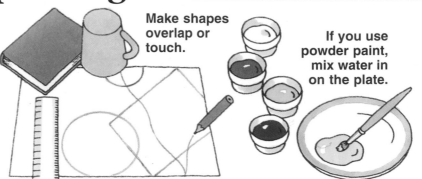

Make shapes overlap or touch.

If you use powder paint, mix water in on the plate.

Draw around things to make shapes on the paper. Draw your own shapes too. Do about six shapes altogether.

Prepare yellow, red, blue and white paint. Choose two colours to blend. Put a little of one on a plate.

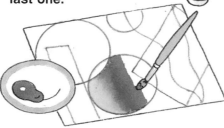

Blend each new colour into the last one.

Remember to wash the brush in clean water.

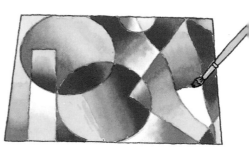

Paint one end of a shape. Add the second colour to the first, bit by bit. Fill more of the shape each time.

Paint another shape with a different colour blend. You could paint in a different direction this time.

Fill each shape with a blend. Work carefully, until the whole picture is full of blended colour.

Multi-colour jigsaw

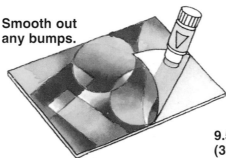

Smooth out any bumps.

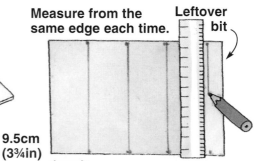

Measure from the same edge each time.

Leftover bit

9.5cm (3¾in)

Do a colour-blend painting, or go to a photocopying shop and get a colour copy of your first painting.

Put glue all over the back of the painting. Try not to miss bits. Stick it onto the cardboard. Leave it to dry.

On the back, mark dots every 9.5cm (3¾ in) on the long edges. Join the dots with a pencil and ruler.

Can you spot where the shapes and colour blends match up?

See if your friends can do your jigsaw.

Bookmarks

Do a smaller painting. Glue it to cardboard and cut it into strips. Cover each one with self-adhesive plastic.

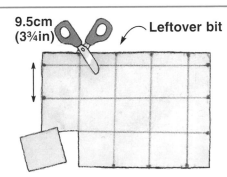

9.5cm (3¾in) | Leftover bit

Mark dots every 9.5cm (3¾ in) along the short edges and join the dots. Then cut the squares out carefully.

Smooth out bubbles.

Make the plastic square bigger than the painted one.

Cut a square of self-adhesive plastic. Peel off the backing. Lay the plastic on the front of a jigsaw piece.

Snip the corners off the plastic. Fold the edges over and smooth out any bumps. Cover all the squares.

11

Thick paint

You can use paint thickly, so that it looks and feels bumpy, or "textured" when it dries. Paint used like this is called "impasto".

On these pages you need:
Paints and PVA glue*
A sketchbook or A4 paper
A3 sheet of paper
Thin, soft brush and a stiff brush
Flour, rice and a teaspoon
Pencil, ruler, round-ended knife
Scissors and a glue stick
Coloured cardboard

Experiments

Draw squares on the paper or sketchbook. Put the paint in pots. Mix a teaspoonful of PVA glue into each one.

Choose a colour. Use the knife and plenty of paint to fill a square with thick, bumpy marks.

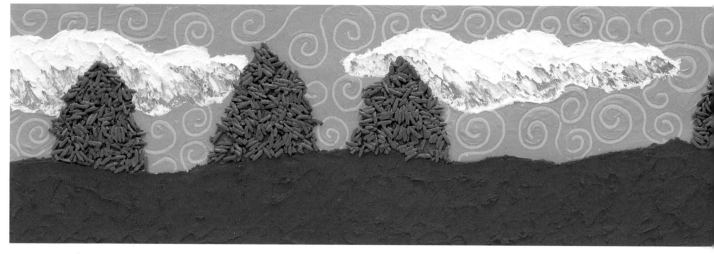

Thick paint frieze

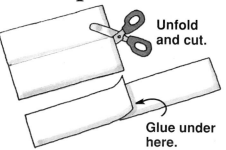

Unfold and cut.

Glue under here.

Fold the A3 paper in half lengthways. Unfold it and cut along the crease. Glue two short edges together.

Mix a pale, runny colour. Use a thin brush to paint a simple scene. Just paint the outlines of the shapes.

Mix plenty of paint on a plate before you add anything to it.

Clean tools before the paint dries on.

Decide which bit to fill in first. Mix a colour you like. Choose one of the ways of painting you tried above.

Textured cards

Make more textured squares and let them dry. Fold a rectangle of cardboard in half. Cut out the squares and glue some on the card in a pattern.

Paint colour onto another square with a stiff brush. Scrape into it with the wooden end of the brush.

Mix a little flour into one colour and rice into another. Paint these onto squares with a knife.

You could make lots of cards in different sizes.

Scrape into the paint before it dries.

You could try painting a second colour onto bits that are wet.

Use colours that look good together.

Now paint another part in a different way. If you scrape into wet paint, paint and scrape a bit at a time.

Paint each part of the picture in a new way. When it is dry, feel the bumpy patterns.

Colour-match spirals

Mixing colours to match ones you can see is an important skill. You can practise it when you make the spirals on these pages.

On these pages you need:

Scraps of coloured paper from magazines
A sketchbook or A4 paper
Pencil, scissors and a glue stick
Big sheet of thin white cardboard
Strips of white paper
Paints and soft brushes
Needle and thread

Make piles of colours.

Tear colours from the scrap paper. Glue colours that look nice together in your sketchbook, in a trail.

Draw a big spiral on the cardboard. Start in the middle and draw round and round about four times.

If you use powder paint see page 6 for mixing reminders.

Draw lines in different places on the spiral, to make lots of sections. Prepare your paints, too.

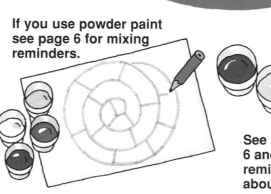

Medium-thickness brush

See pages 6 and 7 for reminders about making colours.

Which colours do you need for making the first one in your paper trail? Mix small amounts on a plate.

14

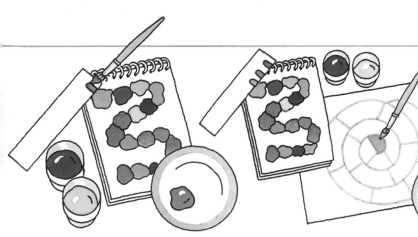

When you think you have made the colour, paint a blob on a paper strip. Does it match the scrap?

Keep changing and testing the colour to get the best match you can. Then paint the middle of the spiral.

Pattern facing down

Knot some thread and sew through the middle. Hang the spiral with the pattern facing down or up.

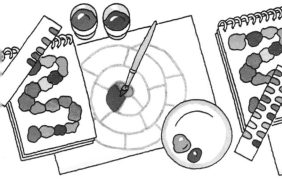

Wash the plate if you run out of space.

Now try mixing the next colour in the paper trail. Then paint the next section in your spiral.

Mix the colours in the paper trail one at a time. Each time you match a colour, paint it in the spiral.

Hang your spiral from the ceiling or a door frame.

Pattern facing up

Thin brush

Thick brush

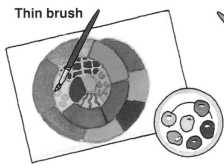

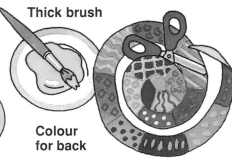

Colour for back

Make more spirals. Hang them on one thread.

When the spiral is dry, paint a pattern on each shape. Mix a new colour for each pattern.

Paint the back one colour and let it dry. Turn it over and cut out the spiral along the curling line.

You could decorate both sides of your spirals.

15

Look, paint and print

To paint something you can see, look very carefully. Make the shapes and colours as accurate as you can.

On these pages you need:
An orange cut in half around the middle, on a saucer
A sketchbook or white paper
A strip of white paper
Paints, brushes and scissors
A glue stick and sticky tape
String and thick cardboard
Big sheets of white and coloured paper

1

Thin brush

Do the shape life-size.

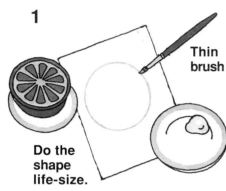

Mix a runny, light colour on the plate. Look at the cut surface of the orange. Paint the shape of the outline.

2 **Spaces between shapes**

Skin

Segment shape

Paint lines to show the shapes you can see inside the orange. Can you see the things shown above?

3 **Try different yellows or reds if you have them.**

White for making light colours

Prepare the paints you need to make the colours in the orange. Then try mixing the lightest colour you can see.

4 **Look carefully to check which are the light parts.**

Test the colour on a paper strip. When it matches the orange's light parts, paint those bits on your picture.

5

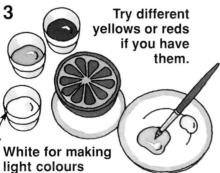

Mix and test the colour you need for the segments, then paint them. Do you need another colour for the skin?

16

Fruity wrapping paper

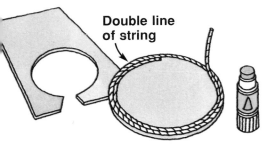

Double line of string

Draw the shape of the orange on cardboard and cut it out. Glue a double line of string around the edge.

Cut out another shape the same size. Draw segments on it and cut them out. Glue them onto the first shape.

Cut a strip of cardboard. Fold it in half, then fold the ends outwards. Tape it to the back of the shape.

Don't paint until the glue is dry.

Plenty of paint

Press all over the shape.

Paint the shape again for each new print.

Mix a colour to match the segments in your painting. Paint it onto the printing block with a thick brush.

Press the block firmly onto a big sheet of paper, then take it off. Cover the whole sheet like this.

Print an orange and cut it out to make a gift tag.

Print a small piece of paper if you are wrapping a small present.

Overlap shapes. You could use a second colour.

Try printing onto different colours.

17

Still life

A painting or drawing of a collection of things is called a still life. Here you can find out how to have a go at a still life yourself.

On these pages you need:
A3 paper or bigger (coloured or white)
A strip of paper the same colour as the paper you paint on (for testing colours)
Different-thickness brushes
Paints
A collection of objects

Painting

1

Decide which way up to have the paper. Which way suits the arrangement best? Then mix a pale colour.

Setting up

First, choose some things you would like to paint. Then find a place where you can arrange them and leave them. Start to place things together. Move them, add things or take them away until they look nice.

Try to have different colours in your arrangement.

You could use some patterned paper or cloth for extra interest.

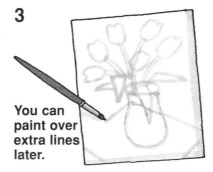

Choose things which are interesting shapes.

2

Use a thin brush to paint the shapes you see. Start with the outlines of the big, main shapes.

3

You can paint over extra lines later.

Then paint the shapes of smaller things. It may help to paint in lines where things overlap.

4

Medium-thickness brush

Decide what to paint first. Mix the main colour and test it on the paper strip, next to the real thing.

18

5

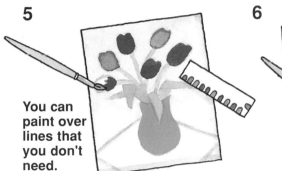

You can paint over lines that you don't need.

When the paint dries, fill in more shapes. Test each colour you mix before you use it. Add a background.

6

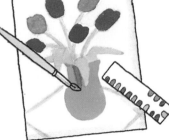

Can you see any shadows? Mix darker tones to paint these bits. Mix lighter tones for light bits.

7

Petal shapes

Veins on the leaves

When the paint is dry, look for shapes and details on the thing you are painting. Paint these in too.

8

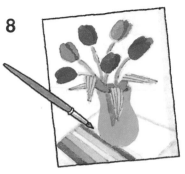

If any of the things have patterns on them, add these last. A thin brush is best for delicate patterns.

Extra tips

Look at the things you are painting again and again while you work.

Mistakes don't matter. Just paint over them when the paint dries.

Leave your painting and come back to it, to see if you need to do more.

Painting people

A picture of a person is called a portrait. Ask someone to be your model, so you can paint their portrait. Make it as much 1ike them as you can.
Or look in a mirror and paint yourself instead.
This is called a self-portrait.

On these pages you need:

A3 paper (coloured or white)
A strip of paper the same colour that you paint on
A sketchbook or A4 paper
Different thickness brushes
Paints
A mirror you can hold
A glue stick and colourful scraps of paper

Mini paintings

Make small paintings of your own eyes, nose and mouth by looking in the mirror, to get used to the shapes.

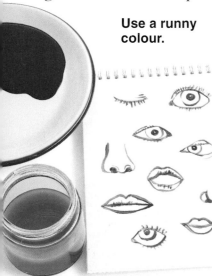

Use a runny colour.

The portrait

1

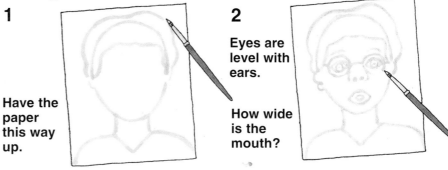

Have the paper this way up.

Mix a pale, runny colour. Paint the shape of your model's head, hair and shoulders. Use a thin brush.

2

Eyes are level with ears.

How wide is the mouth?

Look carefully at the eyes, ears, nose and mouth. Paint the shapes in. If your model has glasses, add these too.

20

3

Mix a colour to match the skin. This can be tricky, so keep testing it. Paint the skin with a medium brush.

4

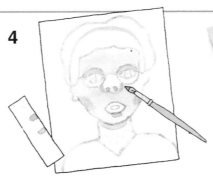

Can you see shadows around the nose, mouth and chin? If so, mix a darker tone and paint in these bits.

5

Mix a colour to match the hair. Paint it to show which way it grows. Is it straight or curly? Does it stick out?

6

Mix the colours you need to paint the eyes. Paint them in with a thin brush. Paint the mouth and eyebrows too.

7

Paint your model's clothes. Can you copy the colours or patterns? Paint details like jewellery or glasses too.

8

Paint a coloured background with a thick brush, or do a pattern. Paint around the portrait very carefully.

More ideas

Make a little self-portrait with a thin brush. Get some copies at a photocopying shop. Cut them out and stick them at the top of notepaper when you write to friends.

Glue coloured scraps of paper onto a portrait to make colourful clothes.

Sponge and spatter

You can make colourful patterns by sponging or spattering paint onto paper.

On these pages you need:

A3 white paper
Paints and a pencil
Paintbrush for mixing
A small sponge
An old toothbrush
Scissors and a ruler
Blue-tack and sticky tape
A big piece of scrap cardboard
Brown paper or newspaper

Starry paper

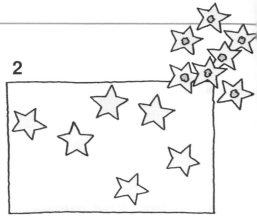

1

Draw a star on cardboard. Cut it out. Draw around it lots of times to cover all the cardboard with stars.

2

Cut out the stars. Put a small blob of blue-tack on each one. Press half of them gently onto the A3 paper.

3

Hold the star as you dab.

Blotchy marks look good.

Choose two colours. Mix plenty of the lightest one on a plate. Dip the sponge in. Dab around the stars.

4 Clean the plate first.

When the paint is dry, place the other stars in the spaces. Mix and sponge on the other colour.

5

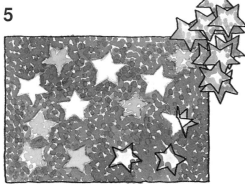

When the paint is dry, peel the stars off very carefully. See the bright pattern appear bit by bit.

Spattering

Spread lots of newspaper first.

Spattered paint looks more delicate than sponged paint.

Dip the toothbrush in the paint. Hold it over the paper and pull your finger along the bristles. Do this again and again.

More ideas

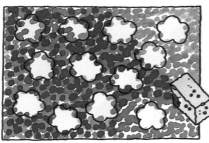

Position all the shapes at once. Sponge on the first colour. Sponge another colour lightly over the top.

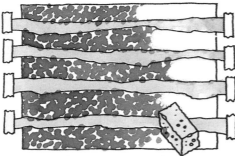

Tear long strips of paper or newspaper. Lay them across the paper and tape them down. Sponge on colour.

You could paint extra detail on top of shapes with a thin brush.

Think of different shapes you could use.

Stripes could go from top to bottom, from side to side or both.

Book covers

Open the book. Lay it on the bottom edge of some big patterned paper. Draw a line where the top comes to.

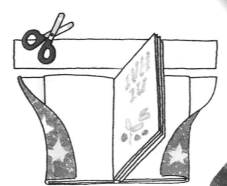

Cut off the extra bit at the top. Then fold the side pieces over the cover and press firmly along the folds.

Painting outdoors

To paint outdoors, take everything you need with you. The best way to do this is to make a painting kit. Take it on holiday, to a friend's house or into the park or garden.

On these pages you need:

A small sketchbook or eight sheets of A4 paper (white and coloured)
Pencil, ruler, thick needle, thread and scissors
Strong shoe box, long cardboard tube, elastic bands
Paints and five little plastic pots with lids
Brushes and a rag (or paper kitchen towel)
Two circles of material (about 12cm (3¾in) across)
Screw-top jar that fits in the box when the lid is on
Small plastic plate or lid of a plastic container

Home-made sketchbook

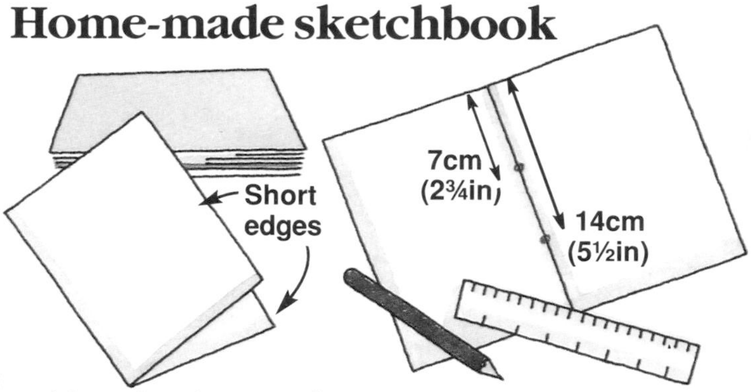

← **Short edges**

7cm (2¾in)

14cm (5½in)

Fold eight sheets of A4 paper in half, or cut bigger paper to A4 size then fold it.

On each piece, mark dots 7cm (2¾in) and 14cm (5½in) along the fold.

Take a pencil for making notes.

Take a small sketchbook or make one yourself. Find out how above.

Paintbrushes go in this tube. Fix a circle of material over each end with an elastic band.

You may need to cut the end off the tube, so it fits in the box.

Take a rag or paper towel to dry brushes on.

Half fill each pot with paint. Put the lids on firmly.

Use a small plastic plate or the lid of a plastic container for mixing colours on.

Half fill the jar with water. Screw the lid on tightly.

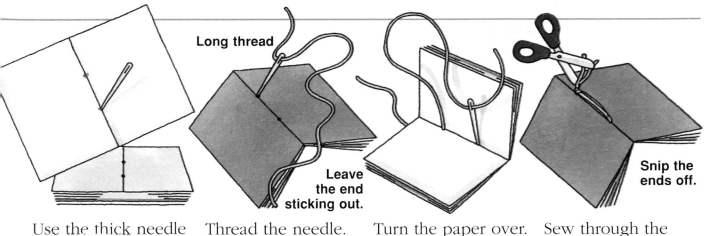

Long thread

Leave the end sticking out.

Snip the ends off.

Use the thick needle to make holes where the dots are. Or ask an adult to help you.

Thread the needle. Poke it through the first hole while you hold all the paper.

Turn the paper over. Poke the needle down through the other hole.

Sew through the holes four times. Unthread the needle. Tie a double knot.

Things to paint

Here are some ideas for things you could paint. Can you think of some more?

You could paint over two whole pages.

Make a picture diary of things you see and do each day on holiday. You could write notes, too.

Paint flowers and insects in the garden.

Tips for using your kit

Use a ribbon or a big elastic band to hold the lid on the box.

Find a flat place to work. Stand the pots in the lid.

Clean everything in your kit afterwards, ready for next time.

Paint and stick

Making a picture by sticking on pieces of paper is called collage. Use collage and paint together, to make an imaginary jungle picture.

On these pages you need:
A big sheet of coloured paper (A3 or bigger), or white paper painted with a blue or grey blended background
Paints, brushes, scissors, glue
An extra sheet of paper
Scraps of coloured paper
Bowls (about seven)

1

Look in books for ideas.

Leave space for lots of other things.

Paint an animal on the big paper. It could be a tiger or another wild animal, or you could make up your own.

2

You need big and small pieces.

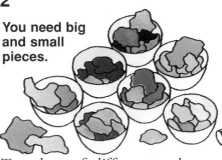

Tear lots of different colours from your collection of scrap paper. Put a colour group in each bowl.

3

Torn edges can look good.

How big is your plant going to be?

Decide where to put the first plant. Tear or cut out big leaves from the scrap collection. Glue them on.

4

Do another plant. Make the leaves a different shape this time. You could use a different colour, too.

5

Use dark colours for shadows.

Add more plants. Some could hang down. Then paint in the stems and paint veins on the leaves.

6

Paint long grass to hide part of your animal, or stick on paper grass. The animal could be peeping out.

7

Add some bright jungle flowers. Paint them, or make them from coloured paper. Do different kinds.

8

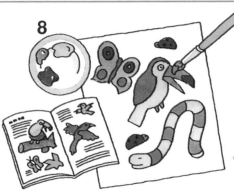

Paint colourful butterflies, birds, caterpillars, snakes and other creatures on a new piece of paper.

9

Cut the creatures out and stick them in the jungle. Add as much as you like. You could add more another day.

Jungle pots

Buy a terracotta flower pot from a garden centre. Paint it to look like an animal's coat. You could do tiger stripes or leopard spots. Stick on leaves and flowers, then paint more detail on top. You could ask an adult to varnish it for you.

Use paint and paper to decorate a collection of jungle pots. Each pot could be different.

27

Computer paintings

Different art programs let you make pictures on the computer screen. The programs do the same kinds of things. These pages tell you how to make pictures with the Microsoft® Paintbrush™ program which you use with Microsoft® Windows® software.

The display

A display on the computer screen shows you all the things you can use to make a picture.

These are different painting tools. You can choose which one to use.

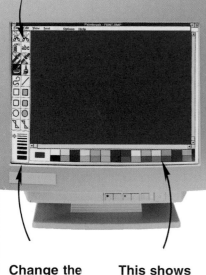

Change the thickness of the mark you make by choosing one of these lines.

This shows the colours you can use. It is called the Palette.

First marks

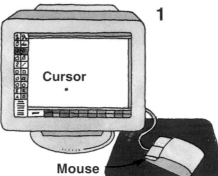

1

Cursor

Mouse

Move the mouse on the pad to move the dot on the screen called the cursor.

2

Tools

Click this button.

Move the cursor to the brush in the tools section. Click the left mouse button.

3

Part of the Palette.

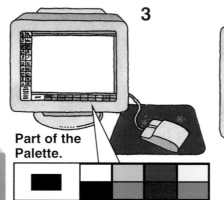

Move the cursor to a colour. Pick it by clicking the left mouse button.

4

To draw a new line, let go of the button and start in a new place.

Hold the button down.

Move the cursor to the middle. Move the mouse as you press its left button.

Draw and fill

Brush tool

Pick the Brush tool, then pick a colour. Move the mouse to draw wiggly shapes on the screen.

Paint Roller tool

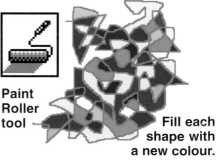

Fill each shape with a new colour.

Pick the Paint Roller tool and a colour. To fill a shape, move the cursor to it and click the left mouse button.

Brush thickness

Line thicknesses

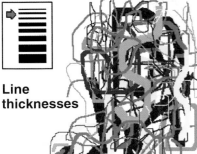

Paint a picture using lots of different colours and line thicknesses.

Painting ideas

Experiment with more tools. Then make paintings using the skills you have learned. Here are a few ideas.

Stormy sea

Spray paint

Airbrush tool

Pick the Airbrush tool. Use it to spray different colours and patterns.

Ask someone to show you how to save your paintings.

Amazing plants and flowers

You don't have to make the paintings very realistic.

Party time

More ideas

If you have a colour printer, print out your favourite paintings.

There are shops which do colour photocopies onto T-shirts. You could get one of your paintings copied. This is quite expensive, but it makes a good present.

Artists and paintings

Everyone has their own way of doing things. Here are some of the different things artists do when they paint.

They stand back to look at their painting. This helps them decide what to do to it next.

They sometimes have a rest and do something else instead. Then they do more to the painting.

They paint over bits of the picture and make changes, until they are happy with it.

Some artists take an hour to do a painting. Other artists take weeks, months or even years.

Artists often make more than one painting at a time. They do a bit of one, then a bit of another.

Some artists paint things on the spot. Others make lots of rough drawings and paintings first. They look at these later, to help them do a finished painting.

Finding paintings

You can see paintings in art galleries or museums. An art gallery is a room or a building where you can see works of art. Most towns have one.

You can find books of paintings in libraries, book shops and art galleries. Real paintings are photographed, then the photographs are put in books.

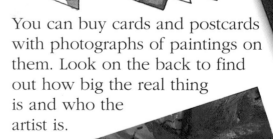

You can buy cards and postcards with photographs of paintings on them. Look on the back to find out how big the real thing is and who the artist is.

Looking at paintings

Here are some questions you can ask yourself when you see a painting you like.

What can I see in the picture?

How does the painting make me feel?

Has the artist made the paint look bumpy or smooth?

Can I see the brush marks?

Who made the painting and how big is it?

Artists and skills

Here are some artists who used painting skills you have learned in this book. The dates tell you when the artists lived. Can you find any of their paintings to look at?

Jackson Pollock (1912-1956) made his paintings by spattering and dribbling paint. Some of his paintings are enormous.

Wassily Kandinsky (1866-1944) made some paintings full of blended colour. They had lots of shapes in them.

Vincent van Gogh (1853-1890) used thick, bright paint. His brush marks make swirling patterns. He often took his painting kit out and made paintings on the spot.

Vincent van Gogh also painted portraits. He painted many self-portraits too.

Paul Cézanne (1839-1906) painted lots of still lifes.

Index

Acknowledgements

Page 28: Microsoft and Windows are registered trademarks, and Paintbrush is a trademark of the Microsoft Corporation.

Usborne Publishing Ltd. would like to thank the following children for the use of their paintings in this book: Amy Jordan, Kate Squire and Lydia Squire.

Thanks also to Catherine Figg for the use of her work.

First published in 1996 by Usborne Publishing Ltd, Usborne House, 83-85 Saffron Hill, London EC1N 8RT, England. Copyright © 1996 Usborne Publishing Ltd.

The name Usborne and the device 🎈 are Trade Marks of Usborne Publishing Ltd. All rights reserved.

No part of this publication may be reproduced, stored in a retrieval system or transmitted in any form or by any means, electronic, mechanical, photocopying, recording or otherwise, without prior permission of the publisher. Printed in Belgium.

More artists

Here is a list of some famous artists. Can you find any of their paintings to look at?

Salvador Dalí
Robert Delaunay
Paul Gauguin
Patrick Heron
Fernand Léger
Roy Lichtenstein
Henri Matisse
Claude Monet
Pablo Picasso
Bridget Riley
Henri Rousseau
Georges Seurat